This Walker book belongs to:

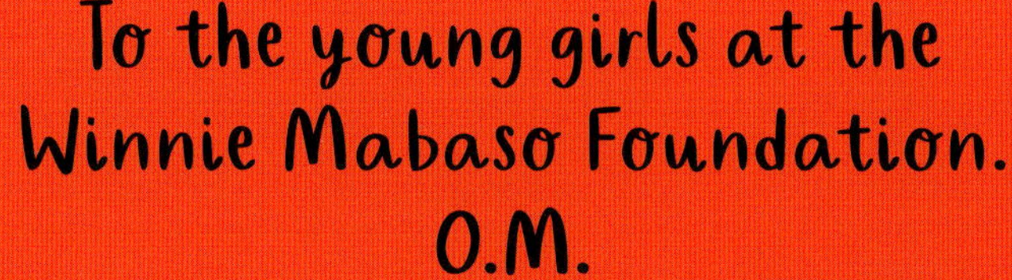

For Fred
S.H.

First published 2023 by Walker Books Ltd
87 Vauxhall Walk, London SE11 5HJ

2 4 6 8 10 9 7 5 3 1

This book has been typeset in DIN Schrift and WB Samara

Printed in China

British Library Cataloguing in Publication Data: a catalogue record for this book is available from the British Library

ISBN 978-1-5295-1106-2

www.walker.co.uk

Oti Mabuse

ILLUSTRATED BY

Samara Hardy

The children were very excited. It was snowing outside. The snowflakes were falling softly to the ground.

"Mrs Oti, please can we go outside and play in the snow?" Naira asked.

"Of course!" Mrs Oti replied. "But let's all make sure to wrap up warmly first."
The children rushed to put on their coats, hats, scarves and gloves before heading out into the cold.

"Before we start playing, we need to learn how to balance on the snow," Mrs Oti said. "Let's start by taking a couple of small steps."

One by one, the class wibbled and wobbled as they stepped onto the snowy ground.

Milo slid one foot forwards.
Then he moved his other
foot, just like Mrs Oti.

Olivia and Poppy were a little
more unsure, but they held on
to each other for support.

"Walking on the snow is tricky," said Umaira, holding on to Mrs Oti.

"How do animals that live in the snow move?" asked Mrs Oti.

"Polar bears plod," said Theo, roaring loudly and stomping his feet.

“Seals slide,” said Olivia and Poppy, sliding together hand in hand.

“And penguins waddle,” said Martin. “They stick out their feet to keep their balance – just like this!”

Everyone started waddling like penguins.

Soon the children were happily playing in the snow, throwing snowballs, making snowpeople and sliding around on their bottoms.

"Wheeee!" cried Ricardo. But Ricardo was going too fast.

"Look out!" shouted Mrs Oti.

Ricardo bumped into Gan with a loud thud. "Ouch!" they both cried. Luckily, Gan and Ricardo had landed in a pile of soft snow. They weren't hurt but they were now very cold.

"*Brrr!*" said Ricardo.

"I'm very chilly," said Gan.

"Gather round, everyone!" said Mrs Oti. "We need to help Gan and Ricardo warm up."

"How do penguins warm up when they're cold?" asked Milo.

"Penguins huddle!" everyone shouted.

The class came over and huddled together around Mrs Oti, Gan and Ricardo.

"This gives me an idea for the last dance for our show – we'll do the **Penguin Waltz!**" said Mrs Oti.

After a hot chocolate, the class were ready to practise their penguin dance.

“First, put your feet together,” said Mrs Oti, “and then your arms down by their sides.”

"Waddle, waddle,
waddle!" said Poppy,
as the group waddled
around in circles.

"Now let's flap our
wings!" said Naira.

"Flap, flap, flap!"
shouted Milo.

"Very good," said Mrs Oti.
"Soon we'll be ready
to put on our dance show
for all your families!"

The day of the show had arrived.
The stage glittered and sparkled.
For their first dance, the children
swirled and whirled around
each other in perfect circles
like a flurry of snow.

The audience clapped and cheered as snowflakes fell softly on the stage.

At last, it was time to perform the Penguin Waltz! The children lined up and the music started.

"Waddle, waddle, waddle!" the children shouted, circling around each other. "Flap, flap, flap!"

But as they danced around the stage, everyone started to lose their places. Milo and Olivia were so busy looking at their feet that they didn't look where they were going.

They waddled into each other and fell on the floor.

"Oh no!" shouted Mrs Oti as the crowd held their breath.

All the children had stopped dancing but Gan knew what to do. "Come on, everyone," said Gan. "Remember we're penguins – let's huddle!"

After a big group hug, the class got back in their places, ready to finish the dance.

The Penguin Waltz was perfect.
Everyone clapped and cheered.
It had been the most wonderful day.

After the show, Mrs Oti gathered the class. "Well done, Gan. You helped everyone dance together," she said, "and the show was a huge success."

"Thank you, Mrs Oti," shouted the class.

"Now let's all have one final penguin huddle together," said Mrs Oti. And the class all gave each other a big hug.

THE PENGUIN WALTZ: STEP BY STEP

1 Left foot back.

2 Right foot to the side.

6 Feet together.

7 Eight tiny steps in a circle on tiptoes, creating a running spin.

8 Left foot back.

3 Feet together.

4 Right foot back.

5 Left foot to the side.

9 Right foot into lunge position.

10 Dip backwards.

And ... **POSE!**

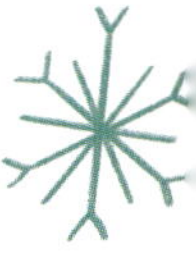

Oti Mabuse is a world-championship dancer and choreographer, best known for her star quality on the BBC's number one hit show "Strictly Come Dancing", CBeebies' "Boogie Beebies" and ITV's "Dancing on Ice".

Oti was born in South Africa and has been dancing since she was four years old. She's one of the most successful South African dancers in the world – and is also a trained civil engineer, which makes her super talented!

The waltz is a dance that is usually performed in pairs. It is known for its graceful pace with smooth turns, flowing slide steps and gentle rise and fall.

Watch a step-by-step tutorial and listen to "The Penguin Waltz" song by pointing the camera on your smartphone at the QR code below!

oti.walker.co.uk/waltz